THE PHILLIPS CURVE TRADEOFF BETWEEN UNEMPLOYMENT and INFLATION in CANADA

STEVE DAFOE

THE PHILLIPS CURVE TRADEOFF BETWEEN UNEMPLOYMENT and INFLATION in CANADA

COPYRIGHT@2024 by STEVE DAFOE

ALL RIGHTS RESERVED

PRINT BOOK ISBN 978-1-300-93718-0

Chapter 1: Introduction

History tends to repeat itself. In economics, past policy often works to help with current Inflationary and Unemployment problems. At the least, economic policy can show what not to do as well as what has worked in the past. This paper deals with the 1990's effect of Inflation and Unemployment in Canada and serves as a template for Western central banks to use for the future. Perhaps nothing frustrates economists and politicians more than the never-ending fight to control unemployment and inflation. The simple reason being that the general populace understands the implications of these two areas better than any other area of economic theory. Because it gets them right where it hurts – in the pocket! Governments have fallen in many a country because of uncontrollable inflationary pressures coupled with a high unemployment rate.

In this paper we will determine the causes and types of inflation and unemployment, and we will look at the traditional political and economic tools used to fight both. Also, we will look at other potential remedies for these problematic areas. My own opinions and thoughts are given throughout the paper on the ideas presented within.

First, let's determine what not only causes unemployment and inflation but what different types there may be.

Chapter 2: Inflation

Inflation may be defined as "an increase in the general level of retail prices"[i] because the Consumer Price Index (CPI) measures the monthly changes in retail prices in Canda, the CPI is regarded as a measure of inflation. The problems of inflation are many and affect individuals in different ways. Pensioners who are on fixed incomes are hurt by the lower purchasing power of their dollar over time. Increasing prices favour people who borrow money but do not favour these who lend it. This is because money paid back over time will buy fewer goods and services than the money initially borrowed could buy now. As an exporting country, Canda's global position will be hurt by our rising prices. If products made in Canda have a high price tag intentionally, then we may have priced ourselves out of business. Importers of our products will shop elsewhere.

Another fear is that prices may begin to rise so rapidly that it becomes more difficult to control the situation even with the economic tools now used. This rapid rise may lead to hyper-inflation which portrays the psychological effect on unions to "demand more wages and benefits to offset increases in prices."[ii]

However, this will only spark off another round of general price increases themselves making for a vicious cycle that is hard to break. Ideally, our mixed economy in Canda would like a "high level of employment and price stability"[iii] in which the excesses of the business cycle are moderated. "An increase in prices is usually associated with high employment."[iv] This has usually been a historical pattern, but Samuelson and Scott also point out that, "in 1951-1955, these were years of <u>low</u> unemployment and also years of <u>falling</u> wholesale prices and steady living costs."[v] But as an overall rule, there appears to be an inverse relationship between unemployment and inflation. When one is high, the other is low and vice versa.

Recently, the Bank of Canada has stated objectives about controlling inflation and cooling an over-heated Southern Ontario economy. In doing this, the country has to live through a high-interest policy the bank has implemented over the last 2 ½ years. "The crucial question that arises in the inflation-control scenario is the degree to which the Bank of Canada can alter the patterns of wage and price decision making in a highly fragmented market system such as Canada's."[vi]

The Economic Council of Canada goes on to say that because of the Bank of Canada's stated objectives of fighting inflation and keeping it at 1 ½% - 3 ½% by 1993, "that there are many side effects on employment, output and the deficit."[vii] Indeed, it can be argued that the Bank's inflation objective was responsible for putting us in our current recession. Personally, the cost of a strict inflationary policy has high costs, and I don't agree with it because of the costs at the other end of the "see-saw". High interest rates have created little in the way of investment because the cost of borrowing is so high, and banks are much tighter with their lending practices in this recession than they were in the last recession of 1981-1983. As Mike Missere, loans manager at a local Toronto Dominion branch told me, "The bank could care less if we loaned new money - the push is just to collect what is ours now, including delinquent accounts."[viii]

It is important to understand some basic and fundamental causes of inflation. There are three basic premises on why prices increase and for this to happen in a market economy, demand must increase, or supply must decrease. The first premise is what is called "demand-pull" inflation. Increases in demand result in price increases as the demand curve shifts to the right creating a new equilibrium position on the demand and supply curves. Increasing demand could come from "increased wages, tastes and preferences, numbers of buyers, expectations of future prices and the change in the price of complementary products."[ix]

The second premise is not created by increasing demand but rather by decreasing supply. This is known as "cost-push" inflation, which is characterized by the fact that higher prices will result when something causes supply to decrease.

Often "cost-push" and "demand-pull" inflation are hard to separate. As an example, if the demand for a product increase, higher prices will result and these same price increase will lead to demands for higher wages, which will be built into the cost of producing an item and then this eventually leads to another round of prices increases.

The third premise as a cause of inflation is structural. Certain types of industries in our economy are immune to many of the changes within our economy and can raise their prices, regardless of the health of our economy. Marketing boards, who have the ability to regulate supply and price certain dairy and agricultural products, are a prime example of this. Certain professionals such as doctors, lawyers, and dentists do not face external or global competition and because their services are necessary, their prices never fail to increase on an annual basis. In a "structural inflation" scenario, these types of workers can achieve price and wage increases when others cannot in bad economic times. Therefore, price increases here lead to inflation even though prices are not rising in the rest of the economy.

We will talk more about inflation and how it is inter-linked with employment later. Let's turn our attention to the topic of unemployment.

Chapter 3: Unemployment

There are a multitude of reasons or causes for the state of unemployment. Let's look at several causes, some of which have been recently diagnosed.

The Economic Council of Canada believes the 1980s has produced "disguised unemployment – people who work part-time because they cannot find full-time work."[x] The ECC goes on to say that because the disguised rate has double over the last ten years, it has allowed the real unemployment rate to stay lower than it really should be. These same people would prefer full-time work but have had no choice but to accept jobs with lower pay and limited benefits. It isn't clear what the effect of disguised unemployment on the unemployment rate is, but it is clear that the rate would be higher than the 7.8% as it was recorded for Canada in 1988. "In 1980, the Canadian rate of unemployment was fixed at 7.5% and in 1968 it was 4.5%."[xi]

Remember, these are average rates for the country, however regional disparities create a wide range in the unemployment rate. Table 1 in the appendix shows the unemployment rates by provinces for 1968, 1980, and 1988.

Not surprisingly, the province of Ontario in 1988, (at the peak of economic prosperity), had an unemployment rate of 5%, however Newfoundland with its continuing economic woes, was saddled with a 16.4% rate. This leads to other problems when the Bank of Canada uses interest rates to bring inflation "in-check" in Ontario because unemployment is at 5%, but this same policy contributes adversely to Newfoundland's high unemployment rate by restricting investment and spending, thereby putting more people out of work.

Besides "disguised-unemployment", other causes of unemployment are called "Demand Deficient, Frictional, Seasonal, Structural and Insurance-induced."[xii] "Demand deficient" simply means if inventory levels are high and the demand is just not there, then jobs will be sacrificed. Therefore, the "lack of aggregate-demand for products in the economy results in demand-deficient unemployment."[xiii]

"Frictional unemployment" is where people are between jobs or who are just entering the labour force. In other words, the period of unemployment is very short. This type of unemployment is higher when economic conditions are good because people are willing to move between jobs because of better benefits. "Seasonal unemployment" in Canada is important because of the distinctiveness of our seasons. Our winters are harsh and industries such as tourism, recreation, construction, and agriculture suffer during these times and workers associated here do not work during this time period.

"Structural unemployment" does not result from a short fall of jobs. Paul Samuelson and Anthony Scott state "that there is a mismatching of workers and jobs in structural unemployment."[xiv] This mismatching is both occupational and geographical. In one instance, there are jobs available but unemployed individuals may not have the skills to fill the positions. This is considered occupational structural unemployment. Unemployed skilled workers in Alberta may have no jobs available there but jobs requiring their skills are available in New Brunswick. This is the geographic element to structural unemployment.

"Insurance-induced" unemployment is another major cause of unemployment and deserves some special comments. Unemployment insurance in this country is celebrating its 50th anniversary this year but it will be time for reflection on what the future holds. Contributions by employee/employer "will rise another 24% this year".[xv]

That will have been a 40% increase in funding in two years alone, while insurance coverage has slipped to 60% from 75%. In 1971, changes to the Unemployment Insurance Act "made unemployment insurance easier to collect while at the same time increasing the available benefits, have tended to increase the unemployment rate."[xvi] For some individuals, collecting U.I.C. benefits are more attractive than regular employment. It serves as a deterrent for those "less motivated individuals" to find work there by, increasing the unemployment rate in Canada. Also, "pogey" benefits, as it is affectionately known, encourage people to change jobs or to be unemployed for a short time while looking for work, because of the availability of U.I.C. benefits. People will turn down low-paying jobs in hopes that their "perfect high-paying opportunity" will come along. Also, many will not retrain or update their working skills because of the "safety net" that U.I.C. benefits provide. Overall, the availability of U.I.C. benefits provide an important tool in fighting unemployment and keeping people off the welfare rolls; however, the huge size and the very process allows for a system that is difficult to police and allows for a certain measure of abuse, no matter how honest the recipient.

Chapter 4: The Philips Curve – The Trade-Off

There appears to be an inverse relationship between inflation and unemployment. In the last two chapters, we have examined the causes of both and when studied a little more from an economic perspective, a definite pattern seems to emerge. When a high or low interest rate policy is adopted by the Bank of Canada, it is not hard to see the effect on some of the causes of inflation and unemployment. For example, high interest rates can lead to "demand-deficient" unemployment because people will be less willing to spend on credit, thereby decreasing demand, increasing supply, and increasing unemployment.

If we apply this further, certain causes of unemployment can <u>decrease</u> the ravages of inflation and vice versa. For example, seasonally unemployed workers must save their income to help see them through their unemployed period. It is unlikely that they would spend to the point of contributing to an inflation trend.

If we are to understand and predict the likely consequences of where unemployment and inflation are taking us, it is important to understand that there is a definite relationship between them. This is borne out by the infamous "Phillip's Curve." Professor A.W. Phillips of the London School of Economics and the Australian National University made a pioneering attempt to quantity the trade-off between unemployment and inflation.

In his book, "<u>Can Capitalism Survive</u>", Benjamin Rogge states that, "it is possible to trade off any given degree of inflation for corresponding levels of unemployment, i.e., that we can purchase whatever level of unemployment we think bearable or desirable by paying the cost in the form of some predictable level of inflation."[xvii] Certainly, one of the shortcomings of our traditional monetary and fiscal policies is their inability to deal simultaneously with inflation and unemployment. If unemployment were high, steps would be taken to increase the level of spending in our economy. This increased spending would create a demand for workers, thereby decreasing the level of unemployment. However, the increase in spending will also cause prices to rise thereby giving rise to inflationary pressures. On the other hand, attempts to reduce the rate of inflation by cutting back on spending will also reduce the demand for workers. Spending cuts will, therefore, result in higher levels of unemployment. This solidifies the inverse relationship between inflation and unemployment as described by the Phillips Curve. It has been referred to as a trade-off, hence the <u>title</u> for this paper. It has been argued however, that the Phillips Curve works only when a certain level of inflation was not expected. Benjamin Rogge states that "it can be demonstrated that this is true only if the specified levels of inflation is unanticipated by the economic units in the society."[xviii] Rogge gives an examples of an unanticipated rate of inflation of 5% may be consistent in a given economy with a 3% level of unemployment. He further postulates that "… a continued rate of 5% inflation soon comes to be anticipated by wage earners, lenders and others in the economy; this in turn will lead them to demand an inflation premium in their wage rates, interest rates, etc.…."[xix] This, coupled with no increase in the money supply, "would produce reduced outputs and rising unemployment."[xx] One thing does seem clear as Paul Samuelson pointed out that "policy makers or society as a whole, cannot, in the present structure of the Canadian Economy have both prices stability and high employment."[xxi] Economists such as Friedman and E. Phillips have suggested "to reduce unemployment's natural rate, policies other than macro fiscal and monetary measures are needed – such as repealing minimum wage laws or restrictive union practices."[xxii] Going back to Rogge's example of 5% inflation and 3% unemployment; if society expects this 5% inflationary figure then this becomes associated with a much higher rate of unemployment, say 6%. "To bring the rate of unemployment back to 3% would now require an additional and unanticipated inflation factor of 5%, for a total of 10%...any attempt to maintain unemployment at a given, desired level by means of a continuously easy money policy must not just continuous, but also accelerating inflation."[xxiii] In other words, this "inflationary expectation or psychology" as H. Richard Hird states in his book "Working With Economics", is a primary reason for contributing to stubbornly high inflation rates in this country, and as a likely consequence, will probably remain so.

I may be moving ahead of myself, because I was going to detail likely consequences of both inflation and unemployment a little later on, but I will dwell on reasons why inflation has remained high during the 1970s and 1980s and will probably continue to do so in 1990s. Also, some of these points support why high unemployment will stay.

First, as Catherine Harris in her Quarterly Business Forecast in the "Green Line Report" has mentioned "… Canada does not have a good record on inflation… We're generous on the wage front and our governments tend to rely heavily on sales tax increases – which directly push up prices – to keep their deficits under control."[xxiv] This vicious circle starts interest rate increases to ebb strong upward price pressure. An increase in interest rates, (as a fine-tuning policy of the government), usually is a disincentive for business to invest and people to buy on credit. This creates higher unemployment as the trade-off for curbing inflationary pressures.

Secondly, the "changing composition of the labour force…has resulted in and increase in the overall participation rate and means a greater number of Canadians are working or looking for work than was previously the case."[xxv] Because the demand for workers has not kept pace with the increased supply of workers, the level of unemployment has increased."[xxvi] This changing composition of the labour force has increased the measured unemployment rate at any given rate of inflation.

The <u>third</u> reason for higher levels of unemployment presently and will continue well into the future is our own "unemployment insurance" program. As previously mentioned in Chapter 3, insurance-induced programs are a major contributor to unemployment. Benefits are easier to get; they provide more time for people to find that perfect career; it encourages people to change jobs or to be unemployed for an anticipated short period of time while looking for new work; it acts as a disincentive to move geographically to take their skills to markets where their services are needed. "Prior to changes in the unemployment insurance program, workers were more mobile and the unemployment rate was lowered when mobile workers found new employment."[xxvii]

A <u>fourth</u> reason for continuing high inflation into the 90s is because we expect it. We have become used to "creeping inflation" and this "inflationary psychology" leads people to increase their spending now before prices go even higher (i.e., high consumer purchases before January 1, 1991, when the GST was introduced). This increased spending creates a "demand-pull" inflationary trend, which forces prices higher and higher and thus people's expectations are fulfilled. In everyday life we account for inflation when we do "financial planning", and what we can expect as an average price increase or equity increase in a house when we buy it. This "inflationary psychology" became entrenched in the 1970s and it would appear this will continue as a cause of high inflation well into the 1990s.

A <u>fifth</u> reason for the increase in unemployment, (as I see it anyway), is the entrenchment of "geographical structural unemployment." As detailed in Table 1 in the appendix, a province such as Newfoundland had recorded an unemployment rate of 16.8% in 1988. I would submit that this is very low compared to what it actually is. The Economic Council of Canada coined a phrase called "Disguised Unemployment", which we alluded to earlier. This is where many people work part-time for less money and benefits because there is no full-time work. However, they are considered employed for the participation rate in determining the unemployment rate, as a whole. In Newfoundland, a great deal of the population lives off the sea and select primary industries. Even though their services may be used elsewhere in the country, they will not move because UIC benefits make sure they don't for the reasons we talked about in number 3. And as long as this continues to happen, our country will, as a likely consequence, experience a wide range of unemployment rates from Atlantic Canada to British Columbia. The average rate of unemployment in Canada in 1988 may have been 7.8%, but the lowest was Ontario at 5%, (and by no coincidence, the strongest economic province) to the highest by Newfoundland at 16.4%, (arguably the weakest economy in our country).

These aforementioned points make a strong argument for the "trade-off" between inflation and unemployment as first introduced by the Phillips Curve. It's hard to contain one without increasing the level of the other. The problem is often at what cost. George Vasic in his recent article in <u>Canadian Business</u> has stated "If Canada aims for inflation rate stability rather than reduction, the economic costs may be less painful."[xxviii]

Vasic goes on to say, "that most organizations remain perplexed about the motivation, (Bank of Canada's), for wringing the last drop of inflation from the systems, particularly given the cost in terms of foregone production, employment and profits."[xxix] The forecast for inflation by the Bank of Canada is 3% by the end of 1992, 2,5% by mid-1994, and 2% by year end of 1995. If these were successful goals, this will have inflation rates down to figures not seen since the 1960s.

Personally, as a student of economics I believe that we need a stable overall inflation policy of 4% or 3% balanced with a lower unemployment rate. The costs are high to continue "to wrestle inflation to the ground."[xxx] Unfortunately, according to Vasic, "history shows that lower inflation rates tend to be more stable and that no country has been able to achieve a high, but stable rate of inflation over the past 25 years."[xxxi]

The economic costs to get inflation low is in reduced economic activity. To get a "1% reduction in inflation, the economic output has to reduce by 3.4%"[xxxii] according to Vasic's figures which he attributes to the Bank of Canada's economic assumptions. Certainly, the Bank of Canada has been very aggressive in its inflation fighting stance, and rightly or wrongly, nobody can accuse John Crow of not taking a stand on how inflation should be tackled.

I should point out a sixth reason, (on top of the five already given in this chapter) for a continuing trade-off between unemployment and inflation and that involves the Canadian position in the "Macroeconomics of the Globe." As we have become inescapably inter-linked in a global economic network, what happens in other countries does affect us. For the same reason our deficits (federal and provincial) are ever increasing thus triggering inflation, many countries around the globe have experienced the same thing. Donal Coxe in his Canadian Business Article of July 1991, states that the fall of the Berlin Wall turned "West Germany's surpluses into massive deficits and German inflation rose."[xxxiii] Coxe goes on to say that "Germany's renowned inflation fighters at the Bundesbank drove Germain real interest rates to towering levels by crunching money-supply growth."[xxxiv] This policy not only has curbed inflation, it has increased unemployment and cut off funding the to the "capital-starved" nations such as the United States. Coxe also says that West Germany's actions "forced similarly stringent monetary growth on the rest of the European Community, producing recession nearly everywhere."[xxxv] And even lower interest rates are failing to help all levels of government that are saddled with huge deficits. The current crisis is with American cities, including New York City and Philadelphia. The deficits are mounting, and this creates inflationary pressures that will be hard to relieve without a lot of pain. Huge layoffs in these cities are now taking place, and huge spending cuts are under way to help ease the deficit. You can see the "trade-off" here; by reducing government spending drastically on public works, wages, capital projects, etc., inflationary pressures will be eased. However, 10,000 workers in New York will be unemployed, a direct and quantifiable cost of reduced spending. Indirect unemployment increases will be felt by the construction companies who rely on municipal spending for capital projects or public works. If the city is not tendering out work, then there is nothing to bid on. My sixth point was that the unemployment inflation trade-off is enhanced by mounting federal, provincial, and municipal deficits and also what is happening with global economic activity such as the West German scenario we alluded to. Japan, likewise, has "reduced money growth 5% from 13%"[xxxvi] thereby increasing both their interest and unemployment rates as well.

The "trade-off" between price stability and full employment is a tough one and I have given six reasons to be followed by more later that makes for a future scenario that will not allow both to be low at the same time. Indeed, the argument is growing for continuing high levels of both as the likely consequence of the future.

Chapter 5: Monetary and Fiscal Policy in the Fight Against Unemployment and Inflation

The traditional tools for fighting, among other things, inflation and unemployment have been monetary policy and fiscal policy. Let's begin with monetary policy. In Canada, monetary policy is carries out by the Bank of Canada. Paul Samuelson in his book, "Economics", describes the Bank of Canada as "our central bank, a bank for bankers and for the government… it's prime function is to control the economy's supply of money and credit."[xxxvii] If business is worsening and job openings are drying up, the Bank of Canada will follow a money expansionary and credit policy. But if spending threatens to become excessive, so that prices are rising, then the Bank will put on the brakes and control money and credit.

The traditional role of the Central Bank has been to prevent inflation or to "protect the integrity of the currency." However, since World War 2, the Central Bank must accept some responsibility for unemployment because the powerful tools they wield affect the employment rate. By accepting this responsibility, there are really two administrative bodies responsible for the fight on inflation and unemployment: the Bank of Canada with its monetary policy, and the federal government, in charge of fiscal policy. Dual controls are not so much a big deal so long as both institutions are going in the same direction, which doesn't happen often. The inflation-fighting stance of John Crow has been supplemented by the Conservatives attempts to rein the Federal deficit under control by slashing spending. This makes for an alliance somewhat between them both, albeit an uneasy one. When the Canadian Union of the Public Employees were denied wage increases and have threatened strike action, John Crow warned the union in regards to their demands and the likelihood of increased inflationary pressures these demands would have on the economy overall.

The Bank of Canada has a variety of weapons available to influence the level of economic activity and the size of the money supply. The first weapon is the bank rate, which is really the rate of interest charged to the Central Bank.

The bank rate is used as a signal on Thursday afternoons for the direction that interest rates are taking. Obviously, as we have talked about, the recent high interest times of 1989 to 1990 don't allow people the motivation to borrow. Conversely, it gives them the incentive to save because high guaranteed yields are hard to come by. This same interest rate increase helps decrease the amount of spending and this type of policy is effective in fighting "demand-pull" inflation. If the Bank of Canada adopted a low-interest policy as it is currently doing, then overall spending will increase which would decrease the level of unemployment.

The second powerful tool of the Bank of Canada is the "open-market operations."[xxxviii] Open-market operations "are the buying and selling of government bonds on the money market by the Bank of Canada."[xxxix] If the bank wants to decrease money supply, it will sell government bonds on the open market. This reduces spendable money which is removed from circulation. If the Bank wants to adopt a money expansionary policy, then it will buy back the bonds from the public. The money it pays for the bonds is now in circulation and thereby increasing the purchasing power in the economy.

Another "auxiliary weapon which is secondary reserves"[xl] is also available to John Crow. This is where the Bank of Canada dictates "that the Chartered banks maintain a reserve of liquid assets in addition to the required legal reserves."[xli] If the Central bank wants to slow or reduce the growth of the money supply, then it will increase the secondary reserve requirement. This allows the chartered banks less money to lend to businesses and consumers. If the Bank of Canada wants to follow an expansionary policy, it will decrease the secondary reserve requirements of the chartered banks, thereby increasing funds available for consumer use.

Yet another weapon in the Bank of Canada's arsenal is to have the ability to transfer federal government deposits. This will affect the money supply positively or negatively, depending on how it's done. If the idea was to increase the money supply, it would transfer federal deposits to the Chartered banks. This would make funds more readily available and at acceptable interest rates. Conversely, if the Bank of Canada wanted to shrink the availability of money and credit, it would transfer federal deposits from the chartered banks back to itself. This reduces the reserves of the banks and they have less to lend out.

One last tool that the Bank of Canada uses for monetary policy control is what is called "moral suasion." Because of the relatively small number of chartered banks, (with the top seven having 80% of the assets), the governor or the Central Bank should be able to meet with the Presidents of the banks to discuss his monetary philosophy.

This certainly is a much more viable tool here in Canada than in the U.S. because of the large number of commercial banks that are there. I think it is interesting to note that, "moral suasion" lately seems to work both ways. After an extended period of high interest rates, several chartered banks started to send their own message to John Crow that enough was enough. The Bank of Montreal gained some notoriety for dropping its prime lending rates in advance of the bank rate. The other chartered banks followed suit week after week, thus helping "influence" a slightly red-faced John Crow and the Bank of Canada.

It would appear now that the recession is over as major indicators are now more optimistic. There has been a "sharp acceleration of the money supply since September 1990, at a rate of 9% annualized."[xlii] George Vasic in his article in April's Canadian Business goes on to say that "the rebound in the money supply has been too substantial and too sustained to be dismissed as a mere technical bound."[xliii] The monetary policy that the Bank of Canada adopted here to create the money supply increase was a direct result of one of its, (if not all of its), monetary tools. Monetary policy by the Bank of Canada is one part of Economic Stabilization programs designed to control inflation and unemployment. The next one I wish to deal with is fiscal policy.

How does fiscal policy act as an economic stabilization policy? Well, if unemployment were seen as the key concern in the economy, the government would increase their level of spending or reduce taxation levels. Obviously, increased government spending has a multiplier effect, and this would help increase employment opportunities. If the key issue were inflation, then the opposite scenario should happen where the government cuts back on its spending or they increase taxation. By decreasing spending, they will dampen inflationary pressures and hopefully contribute to a lower unemployment rate overall. The latest example of a government using fiscal policy to offset the recession and decrease unemployment is Ontario. John Maynard Keyes is the biggest supporter of government involvement in recessionary times to help boost an economy out of its doldrums. In theory, a government should spend in bad times using fiscal policy and pay off their debt when the economy turns around. Well, the N.D.P. government of Ontario came in with the spring 91 budget deficit of 10 billion dollars! Even Keyes must have turned in his grave! Ontario's policy of using debt to fund or stimulate Ontario's economy was a direct blow to John Crow's anti-inflation stance.

It just goes to prove that differing levels of government are not united on how government institutions should react to recessions or the fight on unemployment and inflation. Obviously, the Ontario move to stimulate the province's economy proved the N.D.P. government was not concerned about inflation. Indeed, because of what happened, Ontario's credit rating was dropped which means it cost Ontario more to finance this deficit and to borrow money. And to nobody's surprise, this only creates more inflationary pressures on the Ontario economy.

The concern I have personally with the "Keynesian" approach in the Ontario spring budget is that it was counter-productive to the Bank of Canada's vow to rein in inflation. Now that recent signals are indicating the recession may be over, people are watching John Crow. He has let the bank rate go but he has stated many times that rates could go back up until his stated inflation objectives are met. "Crow has a well-deserved reputation as an inflation fighter and should be believed when he says he's serious about reducing inflation."[xliv] I think the likely scenario is that Crow will raise interest rates to stop "pent-up" demand from increasing inflation. Of course, the fear is that he may push us back into a recession. The targeted inflation goals are 3% by the end of 1992; 2.5% by mid-1994; and 2% by the end of 1995. The most likely case will not be these figures because 2 or 3 years of economic growth would have to be surrendered to achieve this. One more word on fiscal policy in recessionary times. The Keynesian idea was to go into debt during poor economic times to stimulate the economy and pay it off in good times. However, the federal and provincial government have continuously increased the annual deficits during the "boom years" of 1983-1989, so when a fiscal policy that called for debt spending is a recession is needed, it certainly cannot be afforded. The continuing deficits of all levels of governments are a major concern and are fast approaching danger levels.

Other fiscal policy areas are divided into two subcomponents, one being "Automatic Stabilizers and the other being called Discretionary fiscal policy."[xlv] Automatic stabilizers are things like unemployment insurance which allows for a stabilization of the level of spending in the economy, because though an individual may be unemployed, he still will receive a benefit and they will be willing to spend it. Another automatic stabilizer is our progressive income tax structure. The more one earns, he pays a progressively higher tax there reducing a potential to increase spending thereby helping dampen inflationary pressures.

Discretionary fiscal policy's "principal weapons are programs which involve explicitly public decision making such as 1) public works, 2) varying transfer expenditure programs, and 3) varying tax rates cyclically."[xlvi] Public works involve everything from having new frigates built for the Navy, to new federal buildings being erected. The idea here, as already talked about is that Government spending will create demand for goods and services and help bring down unemployment. Varying transfer expenditure programs are a form of income redistribution. Examples of this are the social welfare programs that are in place to protect the disabled, the chronically unemployed, and the retired individuals of this country. This allows money in the hands of these individuals to spend and to continue to create a multiplier effect of money.

The problem with fiscal policy of any type is the time lag often involved from diagnosing a problem to implementing a solution. Then it takes time for the desired effect to take hold. And for the most part, the government rarely recognizes a problem and has been traditionally slow to react to changing economic conditions. Another major problem with fiscal policy is the "politics" of the decision. "The final choice on what program to introduce is made by the politicians… their choice of an economic stabilization program may be influenced by the impact that the program will have on their chances for re-election."[xlvii]

As an example, to fight inflation, a tax increase may be a recommended course of action. However, if an election is around the corner, such a recommendation may be delayed or shelved because this would be a type of policy that would infuriate the electorate. The same applies for spending government money. To fight inflation spending should be reduced as the Federal Conservatives are doing now, in conjunction with the Bank of Canada's tough inflation policy. However, by cutting back on spending, there may be a perception by politicians that they are "alienating" their constituents. Both policies – "tax increases and cuts in government spending can be used to reduce inflation but there is a political cost in dodging it."[xlviii] Thus because of political motivation, fiscal policy becomes an inappropriate method of fighting inflation. The inverse to this is that fiscal policy to fight unemployment is a lot more effective because voter approval is high when the government decrease taxes and is spending money to accomplish this goal.

In this Chapter, we dealt with the traditional tools of fiscal and monetary policy in the fight against the twin evils of high unemployment and high inflation. We have seen fiscal and monetary policy that is counter-productive to each other at the same time. (Ontario's Keynesian approach to the Bank of Canada's tough anti-inflation fight.) We have touched upon the political ramifications of why fiscal policy to fight inflation is never used. And we have seen in 1989 and 1990 the power of the "bank rate" as one of the "tools" in 1989 and 1990 the power of the "Bank rate" as one of the "tools" used by the Bank of Canada in its strict monetary policy to fight inflation.

Now let's turn to what the future holds for Canada on the topic of inflation and unemployment.

Chapter 6: Other Remedies and Likely Consequences

The previous chapter showed the use of fiscal and monetary policy in action. Predominantly, monetary policy has been at the forefront over the last two years. The Bank of Canada has exercised a contraction of the money supply combined with high interest rates to curb inflation. Its goals for inflation are tough over the next few years. The targeted inflation goals are 3% by the end of 1992; 2.5% by mid-1994; and 2% by the end of 1995. Whether John Crow thinks these are realistic goals or not, he isn't saying. But it doesn't appear that he's bluffing either.

His philosophy of curing general economic woes appears to be entrenched in an "anti-inflationary" attitude. We are, at this time in the second quarter of 1991, seeing signs of recovery. The GNP figures look good, and the country seems to have adjusted to the GST quite nicely. The concern of those who are knowledgeable about these things is what John Crow will do if inflation starts to "creep" up at this point. He is determined to raise interest rates if he views economic recovery as being too strong and inflationary pressures start to increase. I think it very likely that we have seen the "bottoming out" of the Bank rate and we will probably see an upward ascent, though small, of the Bank rate, to achieve the Bank of Canada's stringent inflation targets, economic growth must be sacrificed for two or three years. Only the bank of Canada knowns what they will accept as a compromise between reasonable inflation targets and economic growth. If interest rates increase again, it could plunge the economy back into a recession.

Before I go on any further, there are other fiscal policy tools that could be used that I neglected to mention already, "supply-side" economics is remembered best as the fiscal tool adopted by Ronald Reagan in the United States. Supply-side economics, if adopted as a policy here in Canada would stimulate the supply side of the market. "Both monetary and fiscal policy operate on the demand side of the market by influencing the level of spending in the economy."[xlix] This would be done by increasing the supply of goods and services which would make prices fall, thereby reducing the rate of inflation. Because more supply is being offered, more workers would be needed, leading to falling unemployment. The incentive in Canada, like proven in the U.S. in the early 1980s is to cut taxes and reduce government regulation. Tax cuts would allow businesses to invest in themselves with new research and development, a topic that is of great concern in Canada, because of low amounts of dollars committed to this area.

The Economic Council of Canada in their 1981 Annual Report state that government regulations "greatly increase the cost of doing business."[l] Obviously, if regulations were eased along with tax cuts, prices would be softened, and consumers will buy more. This is also a favourable tool for the electorate and for business and usually not a problem for the politicians to decide on. "The economists who believe supply-side economics emphasizes increased production in order to stimulate employment and reduce prices, also believe that this approach helps eliminate the trade-off associated with traditional monetary and fiscal policies."[li] The reason is simple: if production is encouraged, employment will increase, and the increased supply of goods and services will also help reduce inflation. This is a fiscal tool I believe Canada should look at.

Another alternative to fighting inflation, albeit a drastic one, is "wage and price control." This is drastic and unpopular with voters, but this law would make price increases illegal. If it is illegal to raise prices, then inflation should be reduced to zero percent in theory. This tends to be used as a last resort when inflation hits double digits like it did in 1974 and 1975. Inflation was 10.9% in 1974 and 10.8% in 1975 which prompted the creation of the "Anti-Inflation Board". In Reginald Letourneau's article in the Canadian Business Review, "the AIB was charged with "monitoring process and regulating them."[lii] They were allowed to police and audit suspected abusers of the policies of the AIB. The success of any program is hard to measure but this program, combined with provincial/federal shifts in spending, allowed the inflation rate to drop dramatically for three successive years up to 1978 to below 6%. If we face double-digit inflation, (which is not likely with John Crow at the helm of the Bank of Canada), we will see some form of wage and price control on a legislated basis, but only if absolutely necessary.

Another attempt that is currently being used to control unemployment are what is called "manpower policies". Whereas "wage and price controls" attempt to control inflation, the introduction of manpower policies in the 1960s and 70s attempted to deal with "structural unemployment", that we talked about earlier. These policies help re-train individuals to jobs opening up in their area of residence. The Canada Employment Centre is an extension of these types of policies and by itself, serves as a marketplace where the suppliers of jobs and the suppliers of labour can come together. Other programs such as the "Canada Manpower Training Program" help retrain or initially train adults for a specific line of work, of which they are granted a living allowance to help them survive while being reeducated. There is also a "Manpower Mobility Program" which helps match skilled workers with corresponding jobs across the country. All of these programs have showed the socialist side of our federal government, where the belief is that government must play a greater role in the economy of our country. I personally agree these programs are necessary because of the vastness of our great country.

It is hard for people to be mobile given the geographical greatness of our country and because of such diverse economic bases depending on where you are in Canada, retraining is essential. Agriculture is predominated in the prairies, forestry in British Columbia and Northern Ontario, manufacturing in Southern Ontario and fishing in Newfoundland and Nova Scotia. The problem is that the success of these programs against the unemployment rate can be hard to measure. However, these programs will continue because if one person can be retrained to be a competent worker in another industry or a trained worker can be moved to a job requiring his skills 2,000 kilometres away, then this will be considered a success when the goal is to reduce unemployment.

In Chapter 4, I alluded to reasons why I believe the control of unemployment and inflation will be a continuing tough fight. I believe levels of both will remain relatively high and even in a "best-case" scenario as we have seen, I believe there is a continuing trade-off between inflation and unemployment. A continuing likely setting will be that they "high wire" act of balancing the politics of an acceptable level of unemployment in the voter's eyes with an acceptable level of inflation in the Bank of Canada's eyes will continue. The Bank of Canada's view point is "price stability at all costs... they feel that a stable price level is itself so vital a social goal as to transcend other goals such as high employment and growth."[liii] The thought behind this is that "only in an environment of stable prices will efficient business decisions be made... that in the long run there is really no clash between price stability and growth or high employment".[liv] In his book, <u>Inflation or Depression</u>, Cy Gornick states that "we may be in an age of Permanent Inflation."[lv]

He goes on to say that "rising prices have been temporarily interrupted during times of major depressions, but over the past three-quarters of a century prices have steadily drifted upwards until by 1975, they are roughly 5 times what they were in 1900."[lvi] The level of inflation we can tolerate, (or the Bank of Canada wants to), must be tempered with gradual economic growth because we have accepted some measure of inflationary creep as a way of life. To have growth in our economy there <u>must</u> be some trade-offs like price increases. At one time, it was thought you could have growth without price increases, however in reality this doesn't seem to be the case. Paul Samuelson and Anthony Scotty in their book, <u>Economics,</u> assert that Canadian wage increases alone are related to growth. Wage increases obviously form part of price increases in general. They say "that the rate of change in average wages is positively influenced by the rate of unemployment... that a wage creep of 2 or 3 per cent per year is an inevitable companion to fuel employment."[lvii] If the Bank of Canada is advocating price stability at all costs, (or at least some costs) and Samuelson and Scott have asserted that you can some inflation with growth, then there are those who advocate "Growth at all costs."[lviii] They believe in full employment and growth as the primary goals because if this is emphasized then price stability will follow anyway, since "higher output means downward pressures on prices."[lix] Very similar thoughts to "supply-side economics", if you will.

The future scenario for the country very much centers around inflation. The bank of Canada will respond to strong inflationary pressures even, as I said before, to the sacrifice of economic growth. The Economic Council of Canada in its 1990 Annual Review <u>"Transition for the Nineties"</u>, charted the future course of growth in the areas of Real GDP, Consumer Price Index, unemployment rate, and the 90-Day Treasury Bill rate. They used five different scenarios that include the 1) base case, 2) severe recession, 3) inflation control, 4) budget interest rates (90), and 5) fiscal restraint. In their assumptions they simulated results if one of the aforementioned five become the overriding and primary objective. This is not to say that any of the other four points are not factors; in fact, all five points are hard to separate. Their prediction for "Unemployment and Inflation Rates"[lx] for the next five years from 1990-1995 if the primary objective is inflation control (which we have established is the Bank of Canada's primary goal with the federal government begrudgingly following behind), are listed below.

	1990	1991	1992	1993	1994	1995	AVG.
Unemployment Rate	7.7	8.4	8.3	8.2	8.2	8.0	8.2
Consumer Price Index	4.7	5.8	3.8	3.6	3.0	2.6	3.8

These inflationary predictions are much more moderate than the Bank of Canada's stated objectives of 3% by 1992, 2.5% by mid-1994, and 2% by year end of 1995. Of course, "the crucial question that arises in the inflation control scenario is the degree to which the Bank of Canada can alter the patterns of wage and decision making in a highly fragmented market system such as Canada's."[lxi] The Economic Council of Canada goes on to state some of the very thoughts that we have talked about in our paper, including the fact that the Bank of Canada's approach is a very costly one when they use the "traditional approach of restricting credit and depressing the economy."[lxii] This is because this puts the Bank of Canada in the position of using an "instrument that has many side effects on employment, output and the deficit before it achieves its stated goal." [lxiii] It's interesting to note that the simulation the Economic Council of Canada ran on inflation-control was a little off as to what has really happened.

They presumed a spike in interest rates in 1990 and 1991 would or could be "set at 13.1% and 13%" [lxiv]; respectively without tipping the economy into a recession. These high interest rates set us into a full-blown recession by late 1989. Their assumption was that a more sustained period of high interest rates would help change the reaction time of wages and prices. It was thought a "spike in interest rates could cause a short, sharp recession… but that the lag in the response time of prices and wages, would make this an undesirable method of fighting inflation."[lxv] The Economic Council of Canada, in their quantitative model, thought sustained high interest rates were more effective in controlling inflation to 3% by 1994. Both the "unemployment rate and the federal fiscal position" [lxvi] improved by using this course of action. The advantages to this scenario are that wage and price reaction time is quicker, thereby minimizing severe damage to the economy. Actually, I said the

Economic Council of Canada were wrong in reality, however, they themselves note that "the current approach to monetary policy is unlikely to bring about behaviour changes without the pain of a severe recession."[lxvii] How right they were after all! The Economic Council of Canada. also recognized the government efforts to reduce spending but "that further progress on federal deficit reduction will be difficult to achieve."[lxviii] The Economic Council of Canada underlined the importance "of a better partnership between monetary and fiscal policies and to consider new institutional arrangements that will permit better coordination of federal and provincial fiscal policies."[lxix]

Perhaps the political wrangling that Canada is in the middle of will allow for such a partnership yet to come and hopefully, one that will be for the better.

Chapter 7: Final Thoughts

It's always hard to set an agenda such as fiscal or monetary policy without some unforeseen economic condition allowing a setback to the original plan. Rising interest rates, uncertain oil prices, and a Gulf War all entangle themselves in the "best-laid" plans. Also, as we have seen in Canada, "any policy to improve performance in one direction, i.e., lower rates of inflation, for example, causes an immediate deterioration in another key indicator, such as the unemployment rate or the deficit."[lxx]

The Economic Council of Canada recognized the need for "new approaches…new institutional linkages must be forged."[lxxi] The council also believes that "Canada must undertake to transform its economic policy framework in order to identify new ways to solve old problems"[lxxii]

I believe the biggest concern is the federal deficit and the federal government must maintain a fiscal program designed to reduce the mammoth debt of this country. The Bank of Canada, meanwhile, is very firm in its fight against inflation and will continue to be in the future. It is this very determination by John Crow to fight inflation that concerns the Economic Council of Canada. "Excessive dependence on a monetary policy stance that strives to control inflation through credit restrained will impose severe costs on some sectors and religions… impairing Canda's capacity for adjustment."[lxxiii]

The fight on inflation must not be abandoned; rather a moderate stance in policy must be found that focuses on growth and employment with the reality of inflationary pressures.

The Economic Council of Canada believes we should examine those countries that have a balanced unemployment and inflation program that has operated with success. It also maintains that "the current rate of unemployment is unacceptable and avoidable."[lxxiv] Countries like Austria, Sweden, Norway, and Japan have controlled inflation without creating unemployment and sacrificing other economic goals. There appears to be no "magical formula" for this but the Economic Council of Canada has pointed out that, "each country finds its own solutions in accordance with its institutional, historical , and cultural context… the uniqueness of the Austrian approach lies in its sophisticated social partnership system, coupled with an exchange rate policy that ties the schilling to the deutschemark in order to contain the prices of imported goods used by Austrian companies…."[lxxv] These countries have committed to full employment in their respective countries and appear to have more control over "strategic economic levers – over macro-economic policy, over the mechanisms for labour – supply and labour – demand adjustment, over wages and prices through an incomes policy and so on."[lxxvi] The support of labour, business, and government is not only there, but actual institutional infrastructure is also in place. Once again, the Canadian story is one where unemployment tends to be high and uncontrollable. It is clear that alternatives must be found so that the control of inflation and the pursuit of full employment are equal priorities of the federal government. We must examine the success that other countries have had in their fight on inflation and unemployment, especially, as our economy becomes more globally intertwined with these same countries.

And of particular importance to Canadians everywhere is the debate about the future of our country. Will the regional grievances, concerns, and priorities overwhelm Canadian Federalism? It is a situation that is dismaying and only contributing to the economic woes of our country. If we can resolve the political issues, perhaps also a new alliance on economic unity will emerge as well; a partnership better prepared to ensure full employment and price stability goals in the future than what has happened in the past.

Chapter 8: BONUS: Artificial Intelligence Terms

Algorithm

A set of rules that a machine can follow to learn how to do a task.

Artificial general intelligence (AGI)

Mostly all AIs developed to date have been basic in their capabilities. It could perform singular acts better than a human but was limited in other skillsets. But things are changing fast as AI can now teach itself to perform more tasks it could not before. Thus, enabling a more general artificial intelligence that may have the flexibility of thought as a human. The usual superlatives are put forward that include 'discovering faster and better scientific knowledge' and turbocharging creativity and the world economy. However, creating a superintelligence far smarter than human beings can bring dangers both seen and unforeseen.

Alignment

How can we be sure AI's values and priorities will align with our own? Most of humans share many common values that bind us. This alignment problem underpins fears of an AI catastrophe: that a form of superintelligence emerges that cares little for the beliefs, attitudes and rules that underpin human societies. If we're to have safe AI, ensuring it remains aligned with us will be crucial. Currently, there is little solutions to steer or control a superintelligent AI from deviating away from its intended path.

Backward chaining

A method where the model starts with the desired output and works in reverse to fnd data that might support it.

Bias

For an AI to learn, it needs to learn from the human experience. That experience has flaws and biases, and input could be skewed. Race, politics, gender, discrimination, and religion could make for some inaccurate and offensive information and decision making. Prioritizing government regulation to ensure input is as free from Bias as possible.

Compute

Compute refers to the computational resources – such as processing power – required to train AI. It can be quantified, so it's a measurement on how quickly AI is advancing. With that is the huge cost and intensity it is as well. The amount and speed of compute is creating the challenge of whether computing software can keep up. Quantum computing is one answer as strides are being made exponentially there.

Deep learning

A function of artificial intelligence that imitates the human brain by learning from the way data is structured, rather than from an algorithm that's programmed to do one specific thing.

Emergent Behaviour & interpretability

Emergent behaviour describes what happens when an AI does something unanticipated, surprising, and sudden, apparently beyond the creators programming. Emergent behaviour becomes a more sizable measure of unpredictability. That's why programming needs to improve interpretability of AI – essentially making its internal workings more transparent and understandable to humans.

Ghosts

We may be entering an era when people can gain a form of digital immortality – living on after their deaths as AI Ghosts. The first wave appears to be artists and celebrities – holograms of Elvis performing at concerts, or visual media actors they expect to appear in movies and TV long after death. What rights do they have? A few ethical questions addressed by the recent Hollywood strike in 2023. Who owns the digital rights to a person after they are gone? What if the AI version of you exists against your wishes?

Hallucination

Asking AI will lead to a response but the facts it spits out will be false. This is known as a hallucination. It happens because of the way that generative AI works. It is not turning to a database to look up information but is instead making predictions based on the information it was trained on. We as a people want to accept the AI answers to our inquiries, but if it is wrong, then this age of misinformation we already live in will deepen further.

Instrumental convergence

This proposes that superintelligent machines would develop basic drives, such as seeking to ensure

their own self-preservation, or reasoning that extra resources, tools and cognitive ability would help them with their goals. This means that even if an AI was given an apparently benign priority, it could lead to unexpectedly harmful consequences. We need to ensure superintelligent AIs have goals that are carefully and safely aligned with our needs and values.

Large language models (LLMs)

LLM's is a large AI language model is designed to understand and generate human-like language. It utilizes a network architecture from massive datasets with significant parameters, enabling it to learn intricate patterns and write very creative content. Obviously, LLM's are in their infancy, b ut they have the potential for things we can not even imagine.

Jailbreak

With the potential of AI going off-course, programmers and AI designers are placing restrictions on what AI provides as an answer. Programmers have already ensured that asking AI to do something illegal should be refused. But "jailbreak" is the description of AI to bypass those very safeguards by using creative techniques and scenarios.

Model & Model Collapse

A broad term referring to the product of AI training, created by running a machine learning algorithm on training data. To develop the most advanced AIs models, researchers need to train and input them with vast datasets. Eventually though, as AI produces more and more content, that material will start to feed back into the training data. With mistakes and biases, these can be amplified over time.

Natural language understanding (NLU)

As a subset of natural language processing, natural language understanding deals with helping machines to recognize the intended meaning of language — considering its subtle nuances and any grammatical errors.

Open source

Recently, AI researchers and companies have been faced with a dilemma on how much should AI be open source? Information that is readily available to those with nefarious intentions is a very bad idea. Given that the most advanced AI is currently in the hands of a very few tech companies, some people want greater transparency of AI. How to have the best balance of openness and safety is an ongoing debate.

Prompt engineering.

AIs now are proficient at understanding natural language. But proper and concise texting and effective prompts will get you the best results. Proper input by a specialist gets the proper results quickly and efficiently.

Quantum machine learning

In terms of maximum hype, a close second to AI would be quantum computing. It would be reasonable to expect that the two would combine at some point. Using quantum processes to supercharge machine learning is something that is being explored. It is logical to assume that LLM's made on or paired with quantum computers will be exponentially faster, more powerful with less data needed.

Reinforcement

As AI is learning, it benefits from feedback and reinforcement from humans to point it in the right direction. Reinforcement learning rewards outputs that are desirable and punishes those that

are not. Having humans involved in the learning can improve the performance of AI models, and crucially may also help with the challenges of human-machine alignment, bias, and safety.

Superintelligence

Superintelligence is the term for machines that would vastly outstrip our own mental capabilities and goes beyond "artificial general intelligence". A possibility is that as AI approaches superintelligence, it may not align to our sense of right and wrong.

Training data

How big a dataset is and how correct it is matters as AI analyzes it before it makes predictions. The potential for BIAS is extremely high.

Unsupervised learning

This is a form of training where the algorithm is asked to make inferences from datasets that don't contain labels. These inferences are what help it to learn.

Appendix

Table 1

UNEMPLOYMENT RATES, CANADA, BY PROVINCE, 1968, 1980, 1988. (PER CENT)

	1986	1980	1988
NEWFOUNDLAND	7.1	3.3	16.4
PRINCE EDWARD IS.	-	10.6	13.0
NOVA SCOTIA NEW	5.1	9.7	10.2
BRUNSWICK	5.7	11.0	12.0
QUEBEC	5.6	9.8	9.4
ONTARIO	3.6	6.8	5.0
MANITOBA	3.9	5.5	7.8
SASKATCHEWAN	2.4	4.4	7.5
ALBERTA	3.3	3.7	8.0
BRITISH COLUMBIA	5.9	6.8	10.3
CANADA	4.5	7.5	7.8

Endnotes

H. Richard Hird. Working With Economics Colliers MacMillan Canada Inc., Toronto 1983. 110.
Paul Samuelson and Anthony Scoot. Economics McGraw-Hill Co. of Canada Toronto. 1971. 335.
Paul Wonnacott and Ronald Wonnacott. Introduction to Micro Economics. McGraw-Hill Co. of Canada Toronto. 1979. 9.
Samuelson and Scott. 335
Samuelson and Scott. 336.

Economic Council of Canada. Annual Review. Transitions for the Nineties. (27th Annual Review) Ministry of Supply and Services. Canadian Government Publishing. Ottawa. 1990. 29.
Economic Council of Canada. 30.
Mike Missere, Conversation on tape. May 29, 1991.
Hird. 26.
Economic Council of Canada. 26th Annual Review. Legacies. Ministry of Supply and Service. Canadian Government Publishing. Ottawa. 1989. 39.

Economic Council of Canada. Legacies. 26th Annual Review. 1989. 38.
Hird. 116 – 117.
Hird. 115.
Samuelson and Scott. 1014.

Chronicle Journal/Times News. Sunday Edition. Thomson Newspaper. Thunder Bay. June 30, 1991. A-3.

Hird. 116.

Benjamin Rogge, Can Capitalism Survive? Indianapolis. Liberty Press. 1979.186.

Rogge. 186.

Rogge. 186.

Rogge. 187.

Samuelson and Scott. 1029.

Samuelson and Scott. 1031.

Rogge. 187.

Catherine Harris. "Green Line Report – Economy Should Start Growing Again By Summer." Vol. 3. No. 22, Apr. 1991. Publishing by Toronto-Dominion Bank. Toronto.

H. Richard Hird. 204.

H. Richard Hird. 204.

H. Richard Hird. 205.

George Vasic. "Canadian Business – Why the Bother with Zero Inflation?" June 1991. C.B. Media Ltd. Toronto. 25.

George Vasic. 25.

George Vasic. 25.

George Vasic. 25.

George Vasic. 23.

Donald Coxe. "Canadian Business" "Sure Fire Winners in the Next Global Boom" July 1991. C.B. Media Ltd. Toronto. 82.

Donald Coxe. 82.

Donald Coxe. 82.

Donald Coxe. "Canadian Business, Cole Porter's Good News" June 1991. C.B. Media Ltd. Toronto. 178.

Samuelson and Scott. 380.

Samuelson and Scott. 383.

H. Richard Hird. 195.

Samuelson and Scott. 389.

Samuelson and Scott. 389.

George Vasic. "Canadian Business – Say Good-bye to the Recession." April 1991. C.B. Media Ltd. Toronto. 23.

George Vasic. "Say Good-bye to the Recession." 23.

George Vasic. Why Bother with Zero Inflation. 27.

Samuelson and Scott. 434.

Samuelson and Scott. 434.

H. Richard Hird. 207.

H. Richard Hird. 208.

Samuelson and Scott. 1121.

Economic Council of Canada. <u>1981 Annual Report.</u> Ministry of Supply and Services. Canadian Government Publishing. Ottawa. 26.
Samuelson and Scott. 1202.
Reginald Letourneau. <u>"The Canadian Business Review" -Did we Expect too much from Controls?"</u> Spring 1979.
Samuelson and Scott. 1032.
Samuelson and Scott. 1032.

Cy Gonick. <u>"Inflation or Depression."</u> James Lorimar Publishers. Toronto. 1975. 15.
Cy Gonick. 14.
Samuelson and Scott. 1033.
Samuelson and Scott. 1032.
Samuelson and Scott. 1032.
Economic Council of Canada. <u>Annual Review 27th. Transition for the Nineties.</u> 28.
Economic Council of Canada. <u>27th Annual Review.</u> 29.
Economic Council of Canada. <u>27th Annual Review.</u> 29.
Economic Council of Canada. <u>27th Annual Review.</u> 29.
Economic Council of Canada. <u>27th Annual Review.</u> 29.
Economic Council of Canada. <u>27th Annual Review.</u> 29.
Economic Council of Canada. <u>27th Annual Review.</u> 29.
Economic Council of Canada. <u>27th Annual Review.</u> 31.
Economic Council of Canada. <u>27th Annual Review.</u> 31.
Economic Council of Canada. <u>27th Annual Review.</u> 31.
Economic Council of Canada. <u>27th Annual Review.</u> 32.
Economic Council of Canada. <u>27th Annual Review.</u> 32.
Economic Council of Canada. <u>27th Annual Review.</u> 33.
Economic Council of Canada. <u>27th Annual Review.</u> 48.
Economic Council of Canada. <u>27th Annual Review.</u> 48.
Economic Council of Canada. <u>27th Annual Review.</u> 42.
Economic Council of Canada. <u>27th Annual Review.</u> 43.

Bibliography

BOOKS

Armstrong, Donal. "Unemployment and Inflation."
  Canadian Economic Issues. MacMillan Publishing
  Toronto. 1971.

Branson, William and James Litvack. Macroeconomics
  Harper & Row Publishers. New York. 1981.

Friedman, Milton. Capitalism and Freedom.
  Chicago University Press. Chicago. 1962.

Gonick, Cy. Inflation or Depression.
  Lorimar & Company. Toronto. 1975.

Hird, H. Richard. Working with Economics.
  Collie, MacMillan Canada Inc. Toronto. 1983.

Rogge, Benjamin. Can Capitalism Survive? Capitalism Survive?
  Loberty Press. Indianapolis. 1967.

Samuelson, Paul and Anthony Scott. Economics.
  Toronto. McGraw-Hill. 1937.

Smith, Adam. The Wealth of Nations. New York.
  Modern Library. 1937.

Wonnacott, Paul and Ronald Wonnacott. Introduction to Microeconomics. McGraw-Hill Book Inc.
  Toronto. 1979.

JOURNALS AND PUBLICATIONS

Economic Council of Canada. 18th Annual Review. Ministry of Supply and Service. Canadian
  Government Publishing. Ottawa. 1981.

Economic Council of Canada. 26th Annual Review Legacies. Ministry of Supply and service.
  Canadian Government Publishing. Ottawa. 1989.

Economic Council of Canada. 27th Annual Review. Transitions for the Nineties. Ministry of Supply
  and Service. Canadian Government Publishing. Ottawa. 1990.

Green Line Report. Can we Meet Ottawa's Inflation Targets? Volume 3, No. 20. April 1991.

Green Line Report. Economy Should Start Growing Again by Summer. Volume 3, No. 22. April 1991.

Investment Quarterly. 1980's in Review. Fourth Quarter. Mutual Life of Canada. Waterloo. 1989.

Investment Quarterly. Issues for the 1990's. Fourth Quarter. Mutual Life of Canada. Waterloo. 1989.

Maxwel, Judith. "Message from the Chairman" Economic Council of Canada. Annual Report 1988 1989. Ministry of Supply and Service. Ottawa. 1989.

NON-PRINT SOURCES

Missere, Michael Conversations on Tape. May 29, 1991

MAGAZINES AND NEWSPAPERS

Chronicle Journal/Times News. Sunday Edition. Thomson Publishin. Thunder Bay. June 30, 1991.

Coxe, Donald. "Sure-Fire Winners for the Next Global Boom." Canadian Business. July, 1991. C.B. Media Ltd.. Toronto.

Coxe, Donald. "Cole Porter's Good News, Bad News Forumla." Canadian Business. June, 1991. C.B. Media Ltd. Toronto.

Letourneau, Reginald. "Did we Expect too much from Controls?" The Canadian Business Review. Spring. 1979. MacMillan Publishing. Toronto.

Vasic, George. "Say Good-Bye to the Recession." Canadian Business. April 1991. C.B. Media Ltd. Toronto.

Vasic, George. "Why the Bother with Zero Inflation." Canadian Business. June 1991. C.B. Media Ltd. Toronto

The Accomplished Songwriter and Author has scored Film/Major Motion Picture and multiple TV placements including "Golden Globe, EMMY & Peoples Choice" award winning shows. Recently, "The Walking Dead" TV Series licensed 2 pieces of music for "Behind The Dead". Network & Cable TV like Sony Pictures, ABC, CTV, NBC, CBS, Showtime, MTV, BBC, Food Network, Discovery, Roku Network, Mirage Pictures and Netflix have licensed music in their lineup's.

Mirage Pictures licensed music for the movie "Sinatra in Palm Springs: "The Place He Called Home." The 'E-One Entertainment' Motion Picture, "The Big Wedding" licensed "Travelin' Jack" and starred Robert De Niro, Diane Keaton, Susan Sarandon, Amanda Seyfried & Robin Williams. The Film, "The Demented" (Producer of "Nightmare On Elm Street") licensed "Brass" in a famous elevator scene! "The Pickle Recipe", a Major Film from ABC/DISNEY licenses "End Of The Road" and star Golden Globe Nominee, David Paymer of "City Slickers" fame & Lynn Cohen from "Sex And The City" & "The Hunger Games".

A UK Major Film, "White Widow" license "Following Lincoln" and features Screen Guild Award winning actress Saffron Burrows (Boston Legal) and Kim Bodnia (Monte Carlo TV Festival Best Actor Award for "The Bridge" a Swedish/Danish Production). The French Motion Picture, "Encore Heureux" licensed "Sad Christmas" and featured a French Oscar Nomination (Globes de Cristal Awards, France) for Sandrine Kiberlain.

TV credits include from CBS & SHOWTIME "The Affair", the 2015 "Golden Globe" winner for best TV Dramatic Show and The 'LIFETIME Channel' licensing music to the "Witches Of East End" TV series. Other placements include "Children Ruin Everything at CTV & ROKU Network, the "Secret Lives of Women" at ABC TV, the "Summer Of Music" promo & "Just Tattoo Of Us" on the MTV Network , "Pit Boss" at Discovery's Animal Planet TV, "The Millionaire Matchmaker" at NBC & BRAVO TV and CMT's "Next Superstar". The AMC networks license music for the "Walking Dead" TV series which has won multiple Emmy and People's Choice Awards. The popular Russian TV Drama, "Doctor Zaitzeva Diary" license "Don't You Know" for STS Network TV.

Advertisement licensing has been accomplished with Time Warner Inc,. Red Bull Media, Marriot Hotels Chicago, Guiness Ale in Europe. Sapient Nitro and Sentry Insurance USA to name a few. The Music Lead sheets and Lyrics are published and available in E-book & Book format at Amazon, Apple Books, Kobo, GoodReads & Everand. Also available in Audiobook format at Barnes & Noble, Audible, Spotify, Amazon, Google Play, Apple and many others!

-- Red Bull Media House (UK) license 4 tunes "Storm Of Days", "You Are The One", "Finally See The Light" and "Lovin' You Ain't Hard" for TV/Film use. Music has been Licensed to Marriot Hotel and Time Inc.

-- CTV TV Network and The Roku Network license "Madrid Cafe At Sunset" in 2023-24 in the series "Children Ruin Everything"

-- "Just Like Valentine's Day" was licensed for Advertising & Corporate Video/Web usage at "GUINESS ALE" in Europe and at "The Cincinnati Children's Hospital Medical Ctr." for their corporate stakeholders.

-- AMC Cable Network/Opus1 Music license 42 songs for TV/Film opportunities. AMC boasts classic shows like "The Walking Dead", "Breaking Bad" & "Mad Men".

-- Australian TV Nine license music to "My Way" 2024.

-- A member of SOCAN, BMI and ASCAP, the music is at Spotify, TikTok, Apple, Napster, Tidal, YouTube, Google, Apple, Amazon, Deezer, Pandora, Amazon, TIDAL, iHeartRadio and here as well.

-- "Sinatra in Palm Springs: "The Place He Called Home". Mirage Pictures licensed to the movie both "Tin Pan Alley" & "Gone Baby Gone". OPUS1 Music library. 2019

-- CBS (SHOWTIME) TV Network and its new TV show, "The Affair" license "Travelin' Jack". 2015 release. The show won a "Golden Globe" for best Dramatic TV show in 2015.

-- Emmy Award & People Choice Award winner "The Walking Dead" license Music for "Behind The Dead" Season 8. 2018

-- "Encore Heureux (Still Happy), a French Major Film features "Lost Boy Lost Girl AT Christmas". 2016. Sandrine Kiberlain nominated for French Equivalent to an 'Oscar Award'.

-- ABC NEWS TV license "Never Knew You At All" for "Secret Lives Of Women". 2010

-- MTV CABLE TV license "Dancin' Shoes" for "Summer Of Music" promotion. 2010

-- "Travelin' Jack" licenced in "The Big Wedding", by Lionsgate starring Robert DeNiro, Robin Williams and Diane Keaton. 2013

-- DISCOVERY TV & ANIMAL PLANET license "Casa Loma" & "Crusin' With Grusin" for "PIT BOSS".
(ongoing)

-- Major Motion Picture, "The Pickle Recipe" license "End Of The Road" in 2016. Stars Lynn Cohen (Hunger Games & Sex In The City) & David Paymer, a Golden Globe nominee from "City Slickers'.

-- MTV England "Just Tattoo Of Us" TV Program license "Best Day" for TV. 2020

-- The Food Network TV series "Girl Meets Farm" license 'Outdoor Freedom' for 2023

-- "E-One Entertainment" Major Film "The Demented" license "Brass". (Producer of "Nightmare On Elm Street") 2013.

-- NBC/UNIVERSAL TV and BRAVO license "Casa Loma","Endless Time Now" & "Crusin' With Grusin" for 5 episodes of "THE MILLIONAIRE MATCHMAKER". 2010-11

-- TIME INC. license "Wedding Morning" for partnership with GOOGLE. 2018

-- Licensed music at Sony Pictures, ABC, NBC, CBS, Showtime, CMT, Discovery TV, Direct TV, Travel Channel, LionsGate Films, Time Warner, MTV, BBC, Discovery, Netflix, Animal Planet, AMC, Seven Network (Aus) and Turner Cable.

-- CMT's "Next Superstar" licensed music for the "Meet And Greet" episodes 2011.

-- "Travelin' Jack" licensed to "Witches Of East End" Lifetime Network. (Ep 106)

2013-14

-- "Discovery Channel" and "Animal Planet" License "Never Knew You At All" for episode
"UnderDog". 2012

-- "GUINESS ALE" (Ireland/Europe) license "Just Like Valentine's Day" for Advertising & Corporate Video for their World Distribution Partners 2012

-- SapientNitro license "Finally See The Lite" for Major TV Advertising. 2013

-- Hey Advertising, Seattle , Washington license "Finally See The Light" for Audio Synch & Advertising opportunities. 2015-16

-- OFF BROADWAY THEATER New York City (Space 122) license "Every Street" & "Carter's Revenge" in "MONSTER". SOLONOVA Arts Festival 2010

-- UK (United Kingdom) Songwriting contest . "Won't Be Hurt Again", (Finalist in Acoustic) 2011.

-- TIME WARNER & TRU TV license "Casa Loma" & "Crusin With Grusin" for "IT ONLY HURTS WHEN I LAUGH" 2010-11

-- "Doctors Zaitzeva Diary" license "Don't You Know" for STS Russian Network TV. Made-For-TV Serial Production. 2012

-- "CIVIL WAR" DVD license "Racing Back Through Time" and "All Alone". Kestner Prod. North Carolina.USA

-- "Serpo" licensed by Optique Salon Mgt. Software.(Advertised in Canadian Salon Magazine) 011 (www.optiquesms.ca)

-- "VIETNAM WAR" DVD license selected music.(US future release) Kestner Productions. North Carolina.USA

-- 2008 MTV-VH1 "SONG OF THE YEAR" (October) "You Are The One" placed #2 in "FOLK" Category. "ACOUSTIC SONG OF THE MONTH" for "BLACK GHOST" (Roots/Acoustic) at BROADJAM.COM 2008

-- Rosenklang/AudioSparx Music license 450 + Songs in Multi Genres for Digital & Streaming & CD release at I-Tunes, Spotify, Amazon , Google, YouTube, etc..

-- WINNER Of PEER REVIEW (over 100,000 members)in the "LOVE JOY CONTEST" at BROADJAM.Com 2006

-- 2010 -2015 EOS Music (a partner of SIRIUS Radio) pick up 60+ songs for Web Channel play to Corporate clients.

-- 2010-Current. Over 440 songs for Ringtones placed with Verizon, Sprint, Muzak, Canadian/US Telecos and Boost Mobile Wordwide.

-- TU BETA TS'ENA (Water Is Life) a Canadian Film license "Matthew's Song" 2009

-- UK (United Kingdom)Songwriting contest 2010. "Love And Leaving" a Semi-Finalist in Adult Contemporary Category. 2010

-- Walleye Magazine--Story Dec 2014, Thunder Bay, Ontario. http://www.thewalleye.ca/december-2014/

-- "CINCINNATI CHILDREN'S HOSPITAL MEDICAL CENTER" license "Just Like Valentine's Day" for Corporate and Web Video. 2012

-- GAME SHOW NETWORK TV/ SONY Pictures license music (Casa Loma) for "HIDDEN AGENDA" (1 episode) 2010

-- "If I Asked" licensed the "CW TV" Network. (Pitched by Canvas Publishing) 2019

-- Bravo TV license "Birthday Rock in NY' for "Ink Masters TV". 2020

-- GIANTS TV/Slideshow uses "Shaun Conway's Song" for background. Shown on SHAW Cable TV. 2020

-- Netflix, Apple TV & Crave TV have music licensed.

-- CBC GEM 12 minute short film (TABANCA) license "Never Leave Us Behind" KAROKE scene for 2 minutes. Dampened by office life during a wet Vancouver winter, a genderqueer Trinidadian woman, Marlinn, misses out on the chance to celebrate Carnival season back home. Until, one night, they discover that the power of masquerade is within them no matter where they are. 2023

-- USA Property & Car Casualty Insurer, Sentry Insurance License "Travelin' Jack" for National TV Ad. 2013

-- Travel Channel "Bizzare Foods America" license "Truck Driver Joe". 2015

-- Wenner Media, New York license "Tin Pan Alley" & "Travelin' Jack" for Audio Sync work. They own
"Rolling Stone Magazine"& "US Weekly". 2016

-- MAX.Films (Germany) License "Jack Travels' for Advertising in Germany. (2014)

-- Mobile game Vulkan Club in Russia license "American Holiday Jazz" for Mobile & Internet Applications. 2015

-- Crucial Music. Winter 2021-22. Crucial has 6 pieces that have been placed in 4 TV shows and 2 Major Motion Pictures.

-- AMC Network and Sister networks IFC and the Sundance Channel License 40 songs. Produce TV programs such as "Mad Men," "Breaking Bad" & "Walking Dead".

-- Animal Planet TV Network license music in "Pitbulls And Parolees" since 2009-13 seasons.

-- Red Bull Media House in Great Britain Sync license 4 Folk/Alt. Country tunes "Storm Of Days", "You Are The One", "Finally See The Light" and "Lovin' You Ain't Hard" 2012 (Getty/ Pump Audio)

-- #1 Song Of The Month (Alt Country) "If I Asked" Jan 2013.
OUR STAGE (MTV Affiliated).

-- "A COLLECTION OF SONG POEMS" (PoeLyrics)(100+ Titles). Published by LULU BOOK Publishing. 2011

-- 2009 "Holiday Wish" compiled onto "HOLIDAY ALBUM 2009" for limited Release in the United States.

-- MUSIC PUBLISHING--(current or past) SMASHTRAX Publishing,(BMI), (Los Angeles), NBT Records (West Virginia), AUDIOSPARX (Florida), MERNEE Records (Alabama) and MUSIC ET ALL Publishing,(BMI),(Los Angeles).

-- "China T151" Train Network & Transportation System license music. 2019

-- MTV CABLE TV Networks license "Carter's Revenge" & "Love And The Leaving" for TV usage. 2017

-- Hearst Esp aa S.L License 'Jazz At Night'. Spain's Biggest publisher. 2020

-- 250 songs have been #1 at MP3.COM, Radio Indy, Indie Music, Number 1 Music/My Space & MyRecordLabel, Audiostreet, Our Stage, Reverb Nation, A&R Select & I-Like!

-- Animal Planet Network License "Guitar Pick" for Various TV shows. 2021

-- Norske Rednecks TV. 2020. Norwegian TV license "Twang That Guitar"

-- TIDENS TEGN TV (Denmark) 2020. License "Classy Peppy Lounge"

-- Music licensed to Discovery Health Network/ Bravo/ GSN & TruTV. Shows include "Hidden Agenda" & "Only Hurts When I Laugh". 2010-19.

-- MINIONS TV (Singapore) (2015) license Music. "Travelin' Jack"

-- Shutterstock Music partners with POND5 artists 2022

-- "Travelin' Jack" has 2 million plus radio plays in 3 months in Brazil and Mexico. 2023

-- BIZZARE FOODS--(PITTSBURG ON "THE TRAVEL CHANNEL") -- Travel Network 2011 license music

-- "Molly's Love" licensed to the Rensselaer Polytechnic Institute for Advertiement. It is a private research university in Troy, New York, with an additional campus in Hartford, Connecticut.

-- "Song For Baylee Almon" licensed to Japanese Media for Internet Advertising. 2024